# THE EGYPTIAN POSTURES OF POWER

## SALUTE TO THE MOON

### ANCIENT QIGONG SYSTEM

By Jason Quitt

ISBN-13: 978-1544017051

ISBN-10: 1544017057

# ATTENTION:

The information provided herein has been spiritually channeled and refined over many years of practice. This content is shared publicly for informational purposes only.

The meditations, practices and techniques described herein are not intended to be used as an alternative or substitute for professional medical treatment and care. This book does not attempt to give any medical diagnosis, treatment, prescription or remedial recommendations in relation to any human disease, ailment, suffering, or physical or mental condition whatsoever. These practices are not advisable to those who are pregnant or have heart conditions. Anyone who undertakes these practices on the basis of this book does so entirely at his or her own risk.

# DEDICATION

To those who follow the path of spirit to
unlock hidden treasures.

# TABLE OF CONTENTS

## THE SALUTE TO THE MOON SYSTEM

May the Egyptian Moon radiate
upon you and illuminate
your journey.

# PROLOGUE

*Channeled by Light Beings known as the "Divine Light".*

"We have seen the planet you call Earth go through many stages in her development. Some would say that she is tottering upon disaster but we upon the other elemental planes know it is part of the evolution necessary for the expanding life forms to continue on their spiritual journey of becoming.

There are some children of earth who have reincarnated here and now act as messengers of the light to help lead those out of the darkness.

Jason is one such evolved soul whose history began not on this earth but on another adjacent star system. He has had many incarnations in Lemuria, Atlantis, and also in Egypt, where he led the mystery schools of the Pharaohs. Only those of royal bloodlines were trained in these schools.

Saundra and Jason who are cousins in this lifetime were brother and sister in ancient Egypt. Together they taught and healed in the Egyptian School of the Eternal Life Force. They have recognized their commitment to this world and have remembered the Egyptian Postures of Power Qigong. These ancient techniques are well suited for your modern times.

Egyptian Power Qigong has physical healings, psychic retuning, and many ways to connect your life force to the supreme cosmic level so you may fulfill your highest destiny paths.

May the Egyptian moon radiate upon you and illuminate your journey."

# INTRODUCTION
# THE SALUTE TO THE MOON

Welcome to the second level of the Egyptian Postures of Power - The Salute to the Moon. I want to thank you all for supporting this important work. As of 2017, The Salute to the Sun has been practiced all over the world. I am amazed at the results and testimonials this system has brought to my life and others. I have personally experienced amazing things practicing 'The Salute To The Sun & Moon' as my foundational system.

During the first few months of practice, I noticed that my body was feeling sore, especially around my knees and hips. I realized that this was because my body was not used to standing with my left foot forward. During the first year of practice I would hear strange cracking and popping sounds coming from inside my body. What this taught me was that each organ has its own unique energetic field and vibration. When we are doing the Salute to the Sun & Moon we are shifting these fields and bringing them back into alignment. This results in shifting energies and functions right down to our biological systems.

During my daily practices, I would experience many different sensations. The most common is the feeling heat radiating on and in the body. It is as though the sun is right there in the room with you. It feels like I am standing outside on a hot summers day. I believe that we can produce our own radiation that heals and feeds our entire being with the life giving energies of creation. This comes from our internal sun, our hearts.

I have also found that this practice has greatly increased my sensitivity to the energies in and around my body. When I practice it feels like my body starts to breath. I can feel the energies come in through my left side and out the right side of my body. If I bring my attention down to my feet, legs, or arms I can feel the in and out breath coming from that place. This is an amazing feeling that has taken me years to build up to. It is as if my body is breathing the pure energies of the universe.

I have found that adding crystals and essential oils to my practice has greatly amplify and enhance my experience. Using pharaoh cylinders, essential oils or quartz crystals before the postures can assist in opening your channels and energetic bodies to the universal energies. In my healing room, I also place many quartz crystals and set the intention for healing and spiritual growth. Practicing with these tools and setting the right intentions can greatly enhance the The Egyptian Postures of Power.

There was a time when I would practice the Salute to the Sun nine times a day. I know this is a little extreme but I wanted to see what effect it would have on me.

The results were amazing, I found myself only needing 3-4 hours of sleep a night and I would wake up completely energized feeling full of life. It also greatly enhanced my dreaming to a point where I would be able to remember all my dreams in great details. It would feel as if I was dreaming for days.

The only problem with this was I would go to sleep around 11pm and wake up around 3am ready to start my day. This type of schedule did not fit my lifestyle so I went back down to practicing the Salute To The Sun one to three times a day at the most.

Think of each posture as a unique vibration that creates an energetic field around the body. When done in a specific order you are building unique energetic structures around and within your body. These vibrations are like a harmonic code sending music out into the cosmos. This not only attunes you to a higher source of energy but sets up the energies you will attract during the day. When I am not in the of best moods or feeling down the best remedy I could do is practice the Salute to the Sun & Moon. After I instantly feel that my energy has shifted and I feel completely rejuvenated. If you are a health care provider and see many clients a day, doing exercises like these can help keep you from burning yourself out. Also, it protects and strengthens your energies so that you do not pick up the energies of your clients. If you do pick something up from your clients, simply do the postures again to cleanse yourself of their energies.

You can see how these postures can make their way into your daily rituals, just like brushing your teeth!

# THE WEIGHING OF THE HEART

I believe that we are here in this life to experience our purpose and live out our karma so we may evolve and ascend into higher planes of existence. We do this by processing our life experiences through our chakra and energy systems. When one holds onto past experiences, thought forms, traumas, emotions, etc, they unknowingly weigh down and cause havoc on current life situations and future life paths. This is what we call Karma. Everything has a vibration, be it a thought or an emotion, when we store these vibrations in our bodies we attract the same vibrations towards us on our life paths. For example, if someone is always angry, they will bring energies of anger into their path that will keep them in a state of anger.

The ancient Egyptians believed that when you died your spirit would be brought to the throne of the gods to be judged. This was done by weighing the heart of the deceased on a scale with the feather of truth. If your heart was heavier then the feather you were sent back to the world to try again. If your heart was equal the feather you were given a choice to ascend to become one of the gods or go back into the world as a pharaoh representing the gods.

This belief is very interesting, its purpose was to teach that what you carry in your heart determines your life path. If you carry fear, anger, guilt, hate, etc, you would not ascend. Only a pure heart that carries truth and love will be on the right path. This is why it is so important to not only understand these concepts but understand how we can release the energies that we carry. The Egyptian Postures of Power are one of the ways we can shift and move these energies out of our physical, emotional, mental and spiritual bodies. By practicing these movements, we are consciously moving and releasing lifetimes of heavy and stagnant energies that are holding us in negative patterns.

The more we practice the more we shift and refine our energies so we may move into higher realms of experience.

# THE HISTORY OF THE EGYPTIAN POSTURES

The history of the postures goes back many eons, dimensions and star systems. The postures were originally brought to our ancestors from the Pleiades Star System and were used in the time of Atlantis when the world started to move out of its natural order.

These postures were channeled to us by the original star ancestors that brought mankind to earth. The purpose of the postures was to change the vibrational nature of human and planetary consciousness to prevent future catastrophes. Since the human race is once again heading down this path, these postures have been brought back to help those that practice to escape the negative influences and shift the environment around them. Through individual practice these postures have the power to teach the secrets of ascension.

The postures have been reformulated for the human nervous system. This is because each civilization has been slightly modified.

The ones that are ready to receive these energies will be easily drawn to these teachings and frequencies.

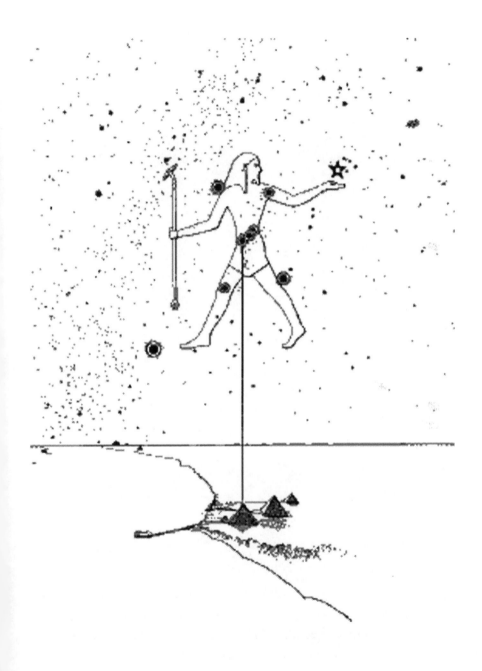

# THE SALUTE TO THE MOON

The Salute to the Moon connects you to the next level of consciousness that is outside of your physical, mental, emotional and spiritual bodies. This level connect you beyond the cosmos to energies of conscious evolution and prepares your transition into future lives.

This is a very advanced system that can only be practiced after one is well versed in the energies of The Salute to the Sun. It is very important that you build a strong foundation with The Salute to the Sun before moving into the Moon Postures.

Just as The Salute to the Sun works with highest level of planetary, physical, emotional and spiritual energies. The Salute to the Moon is preparing your energies for the transition into your future incarnations in other dimensions and planetary systems. It builds upon the energies Salute to the Sun to enhance your spiritual awareness, creativity and helps move you along your path gently releasing energetic obstacles in your way.

The Salute to the Moon can be practiced anytime, but is most potent when practiced the nights of the new and full moon.

# THE SUN & MOON

In ancient times, religious practices were based around the cycles of the Sun and Moon. In fact most major religions today are still based on these cycles. It was important for an ancient culture to understand these cycles in order to know when to plant and when to harvest. Many religious festivals are still carried out today on the days of the year to celebrate the planting of seeds and the harvesting of the food. In Egypt these cycles were also timed with the flooding of Nile river.

The understanding of these concepts were of life and death to an ancient culture because if you planted your crops at the wrong time you wouldn't be able to feed your family for the next year.

The Sun provided light, energy, warmth, growth and life to all things on the planet. Where as the moon was domain of the waters, the unconscious, death and darkness. The energies of the moon has an interesting effect on our bodies, minds and emotions. On a full moon the body seems to retain more water weight and many people experience heightened emotions.

People are more likely to go to the hospital, get in accidents or get arrested on full moons. We even call crazy people 'lunatics' referring to the moons effect on the mind. The moon is also reflected in the human hand, you can count the 28 day moon cycle using the 14 division on each hand. This is also the reflected in the 28 day menstruation cycle of women. This is the reason that moon goddesses of the past were also viewed as gods of fertility. The Sun and the Moon personified the perfect archetypes of male and female polarities.

The Sun - Right Eye
Masculine Polarity
Connected to Left Brain
Power - Logical

The Moon - Left Eye
Feminine Polarity
Connected to Right Brain
Spiritual - Creative

In Egypt Isis was associated as the moon goddess having control over the currents of the oceans, we can still see this influence in our language today. When we put the word ISIS together we get the symbol of the dollar sign $, thats why we call it 'Mon'ey. She controls the currents of the oceans, thats why we call money 'currency'. Finally the water currents create the 'Banks' on the shores. Its amazing to see the influence ancient ideas subconsciously have on our language.

The energy of the moon is very potent because it is the combination of the energies of the sun being reflected off the surface of the moon. If you picture the suns energy as a warm golden fire then the energies of the moon can be seen as a celestial silver fire. The energies of this cosmic fire builds up every month peaking at the full moon. This is why special ceremonies were reserved on the nights of the full moon when the energies were at its most potent. They say when you plant an intention or goal on the new moon, it will grow and come to fruition on the full moon.

You may also notice that great inspiration, dreams, journeys and spiritual experiences often happen around the full moon. This is because the moon carries with it a strong connection to our unconscious. When its full we can better perceive things that are hidden deep within us. We are also more naturally psychic around the time of the full moon, many healers also find that their healing ability are greatly amplified.

In ancient Egypt hyssop oil was used by the priests to connect to the celestial energies. They did this by placing the hyssop oil on the inside of their elbows and behind the knees on the new and full moon. This is to help them ground the energies of the moon and be in alignment with the celestial cycles.

# FOOT POSTURES

The artwork of ancient Egypt depicted the gods, pharaohs and common people in very specific foot postures. These stances held great meaning and importance to these artists in capturing the energy they wanted to portray. Most statues are depicted with the left foot forward and this stance is also the first posture in the Salute to the Sun.

When the left foot is forward it connects you to the universe around you. When the right foot is forward you are bringing the energies of the universe in your body. When we stand with our feet together we are creating our own personal space and when our feet are apart we are grounding these energies into the earth.

As you can see, the stance we choose can greatly effect what kind of energy we want flowing through our bodies.

**Beginning of the journey**
Left foot forward
Connecting to the universe

**Moving through time**
Right foot forward
Bringing the universe within

**Standing in the sacred spot**
Feet together
Creates a pyramid of protection around the body

**Stance of mankind**
Feet shoulder width apart
Grounds and holds the energies

# THE SALUTE TO THE MOON POSTURES

# CONNECTING THE EARTH & HEART

(1) Place feet together, hands open to the side. Feel the energies of the Earth under you. This is the posture for grounding.

(2) Focus on feeling the energies of your body connecting to the energies of the Earth. Rotate your palms to face forward.

(3) Bring your hands up to your heart in prayer posture. Your heart connects you out to the entire universe. Feel the energies of your heart reaching out to the Universe. This motion joins the energies of your heart and the Earth together as one.

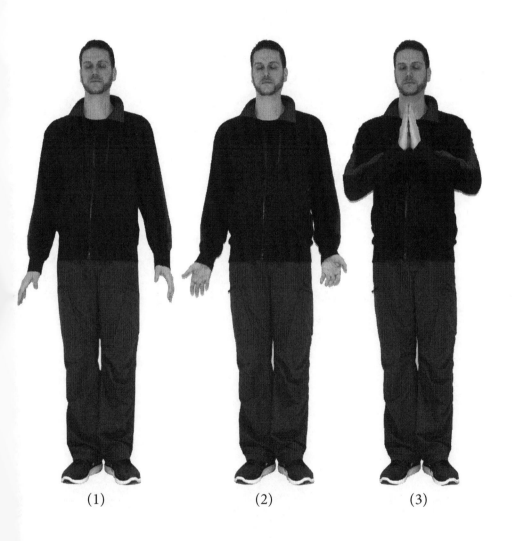

(1)                    (2)                    (3)

# SALUTING THE HEAVENS

(1) Rise your arms up with your palms facing forward to salute the heavens. Feel the heavenly energies opening the channels of your body.

(2) Rotate your palms slightly so that your hands are facing the sky. Feel the connection between the energies of the heavens and the energies of your body.

(1)                                    (2)

# SALUTE TO THE MOON

(1-4) Bring your hands together in the Moon mudra above your head. This mudra connects to the energies of the Moon and allows these energies to flow down through your entire body.

These lunar energies are much more refined then solar energy.

Slowly bring this mudra down your body stopping at each chakra.

Feel the lunar energies opening and filling your chakras with the celestial energies.

(1) (2)

(3) (4)

# SALUTE TO THE MOON
## CONTINUED...

(5-8) As your hands reach down to the solar plexus, slowly rotate your hands so that the Moon murda is now facing downward.

Continue to bring this mudra down the rest of your chakras.

(5)

(6)

(7)

(8)

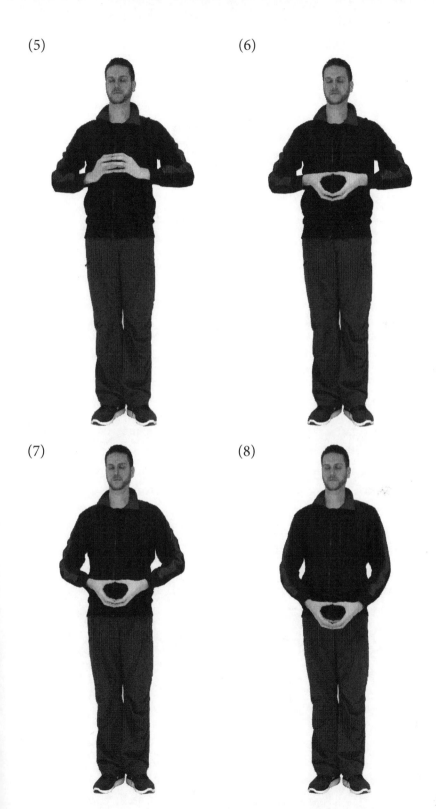

# SALUTE TO THE MOON CONTINUED...

(9-14) Bring the moon energies down the knees to your feet.

Open your hands and let your fingers touch the ground in front of you. This grounds these energies into the earth.

As you slowly begin to stand back up, bring the energies of the earth and the moon up your legs and into your body.

When you are fully standing up your hands should be at your sides.

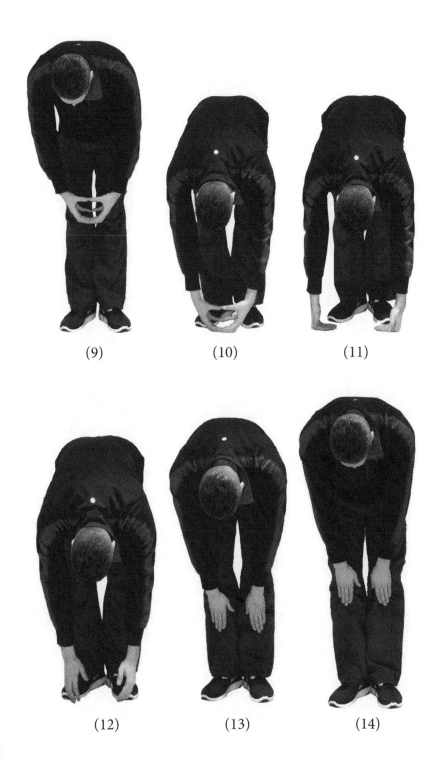

(9)  (10)  (11)

(12)  (13)  (14)

# FLIGHT OF THE PHOENIX

(1) With your hands at your side, open palms to face the ground.

(2) Slowly raise your arms out from your sides until they are above your head. This posture brings the fire energies into the body.

(3) Hold this position to open your channels and meridians.

(1)

(2)

(3)

# FLIGHT OF THE PHOENIX
## CONTINUED...

(4-5) Bring arms down until they are parallel to the ground then slowly lift them back above your head.

Repeat this motion at least six times. This action opens and expands the auric field out into the environment connecting you with the spider webs of Earth energy.

(4)

(5)

# THE HALL OF RECORDS

(1) Turn hands to face the heaven and slowly raise your arms to over you head.

(2) Connect your fingers into the Moon mudra.

(3) Slightly raise your arms up and down above your head. This action brings information down from the higher realms that is vital for your own personal growth.

(1)

(2)

(3)

# THE HALL OF RECORDS CONTINUED...

(4) Bring down the Moon mudra to behind your head.

(5) Slowly raise your arms back up to above your head, palms facing forward.

(4)                              (5)

# HORNS OF THE GODS

(1) Slowly bring your arms down your side with your palms facing forward.

(2) As they reach the Sacral Chakra cross arms with palms facing up. The right arm should be on top of the left.

(3) Then slowly raise your arms to above your head. This mingles the energies of the body to harmonize your polarities.

(4) Turn Palms to face the ground and then open your legs to shoulder width apart.

(5) Open your arms to the side. From this stance you can then bring your arms back down to their sides.

(1)

(2)

(3)

(4)

(5)

# HIGHWAY OF THE GODS

(1) Open legs to shoulder width apart with arms out to the sides, palms facing the ground.

(2) Place your body weight on your right leg and slowly rotate hands to face the heavens.

This action works with healing the air element and the environment around you. Connects the energies of channeling and clearing into the Higher chakras.

(1)

(2)

# HIGHWAY OF THE GODS
## CONTINUED...

(3) Move your body weight on your left leg hands facing the ground.

(4) Slowly rotate to face the heavens.

(3)

(4)

# HIGHWAY OF THE GODS CONTINUED...

(5) Move back to center, hands facing the ground.

(6) Slowly rotate to face the heavens.

(5)

(6)

# HANDS OF TRANSPARENCY

(1) Bring your arms down to behind your back. Place the back of your hands over your kidney area.

(2-3) Sweep your hands out to the front of your solar plexus then slowly push your hands out in front of you.

This is a powerful meditation posture which allows higher energies and knowledge to flow through your body.

(1)                    (2)                    (3)

# HANDS OF TRANSPARENCY
## CONTINUED...

(4-9) Bring the energy down your left leg. Touch the ground and sweep the energy over and back up your right leg.

(4)     (5)     (6)

(7)     (8)     (9)

# THE DIAMOND ZONE

(1) Raise your palms in front of your Sacral Chakra.

(2) Place your hands into the cradle of life mudra. This clears and builds energy into your Sacral Chakra.

(3) Bring your feet together after before moving into the next posture.

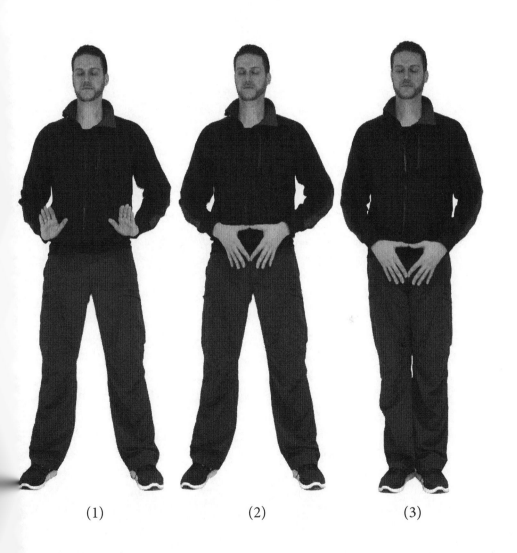

(1)                    (2)                    (3)

# THE CUP OF ISIS

(1) Raise your arms above your head, hands facing the sky.

(2) Rotate your palms from front to back at least six times.

(3) Then bring your hands together into the cup of Isis mudra. This allows the solar and lunar energies to flow down throughout the body.

(4) Bring the cup of Isis down the front of the body to over the heart. Put fingers together in the Moon mudra over the heart. This brings the energies down into the heart to assists in manifesting new energies and creative ideas.

(1)

(2)

(3)

(4)

59

# THE WINGS OF RA

(1) Place your legs shoulder width apart and your arms parallel to the ground with palms facing down.

(2) Slowly rotate your palms so they face the sky.

(3) Bring your feet back together then slowly bring your hands over your heart in prayer mudra. This posture unites all the energies of the body in one stream of awareness.

This posture concludes the Salute To The Moon postures.

(1)

(2)

(3)

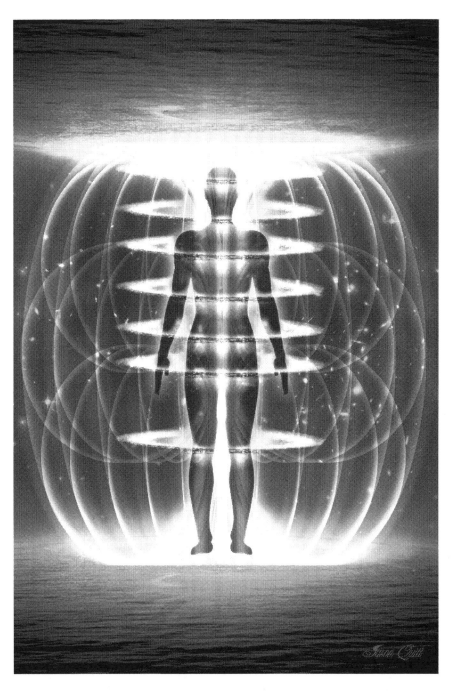

Jason Quitt's original artwork of the energy bodies.

Jason Quitt's original artwork of the chakra systems.

# Jason Quitt Biography

Jason would be considered a life long experiencer who has interacted with the multidimensional worlds.

Since an early age Jason has been awakened to things that are outside the normal range of perception of just the physical world. He has had many out of body experiences and has encountered ghosts, aliens and other dimensional beings. He has been taken on out of body time travel journeys and has remembered many of his past lives.

"In my early 20's, I started having terrifying experiences of sleep paralysis. I would be awakened by a presence in my room but I would be frozen and unable to wake myself up. These experiences started to happen more frequently and I started to become more and more conscious of what was going on. One night as I was trying very hard to shake myself out of this paralysis, something happened I wasn't expecting. I shook myself so hard that I popped out of my body and had my first out-of-body experience. As I came out of my body, I could see myself lying in bed frozen and there was a very tall being standing at the end of my bed. I knew that this was a genuine experience and was beyond my comprehension. From that moment on my perception of this world has shifted.

Ever since my first out-of-body experience, I found that under the right conditions I could leave my body and start to explore these new dimensions that had been opened to me. As I started to venture out into these new worlds, many different beings, guides, masters and energies started to come into my life. They would often wake me up and take me out of my body on journeys to many places and time lines to show and teach me many new things. I was no longer the same person after experiencing these journeys.

These beings gave me specific teachings to follow so I may live comfortably in this world. They said that the most important thing is to heal yourself, and only then could I effect change in others. Under their teachings and guidance I sought out many teachers and masters to receive wisdom and healing. Since then I have been given many powerful healing techniques and abilities to assist myself and others on the many paths of healing and enlightenment. "

Since then, Jason has been studying various modalities and spiritual practices with teachers from around the world. He graduated from the Institute of Energy Wellness in 2005 and began working with ancient healing techniques and became a student of Algonquin Shamanism. From his out of body experiences Jason has received information on numerous energetic systems of healing and spiritual development. He published these methods in his book "Egyptian Postures of Power - Ancient Qigong System" and "The Yosef Codes - Sacred Geometry Mandalas".

In 2015, Jason started to work on publishing his story and information with the late Bob Mitchell. "Forbidden Knowledge - Revelations of a Multidimensional Time Traveler" was released March 2016, and almost instantly went international being translated into German, Chinese and Japanese. Jason was also one of the guest personalities featured in the 2015 UFO documentary "The Resonance". Jason has also worked as the creative director for Tesla Magazine from 2014-15.

Made in the USA
Middletown, DE
24 April 2017